SLIGHTLY DAMAGED;
TOTALLY DIVINE

SLIGHTLY DAMAGED; TOTALLY DIVINE

A Book of Poems

MEGHANN BIRKS

Meghann Birks

Dedicated to Elliot and Louie,
the reason I take risks like this.

To Andrew,
who encourages me to Seize the Carp.

And to my mother, Margaret Brown.
I find myself at a loss for words as to how you have shaped me,
but know that I would not be who I am were I not your daughter.

I'm so grateful that I chose
you to be my mom.

Copyright © 2021 by Meghann Birks

All rights reserved. No part of this book may be reproduced in any manner whatsoever without written permission except in the case of brief quotations embodied in critical articles and reviews.

First Printing, 2021

CONTENTS

Foreword	1
A Revelatory Tale	5
Enough	9
When They Howl	13
Stardust	17
A Knock on the Door After Dark	19
How Jarring It Is to Look Into the Mirror	21
This Middle Aged Rage	23
Sturdy	27
Wild Thing	29
Slightly Damaged And Totally Divine	31
Two Women	33
Reckoning	35
Eve; Reimagined	37
I Am Loving Myself Whole	39
There is Joy to Be Had	41

Climb	43
Oh Captain, School Captain!	45
If I Could Swallow Fire	47
Wonder	49
What Story Do You Tell Yourself?	51
This Grief	55
Treadmill (a haiku)	57
I Was Raised by the Ocean	59
Swiss Army Soul	61
Psych Ward	63
Antidote	65
Undammed	67
Waiting for Later	69
Doris	71
Psychic	73
Umbrella	75
The Audacious Berry	77
Solitude	79
Wildness	81
Return to Earth	83
Hemlock	85
Surrender	87

My Grandmother's Kitchen	89
Green Beans	91
Absurdity	93
Strawberries	95
Roots	97
About The Author	99

Foreword

There are 42 poems in this book because it is my gift to myself on my 42nd birthday. Self- indulgent, perhaps. But I've spent most of my life indulging other people, so why not me?

I've been a creative and a poet my entire life, though I kept it hidden for a good long while as I tried to fly under the radar. But the year I turned 40, I had a midlife revelation when I realised that (if I'm lucky) I have as many years ahead as there are behind me. Certainly, my liver and heart may put in for early retirement which would be disappointing, but understandable.

A few months after the milestone birthday, while I was tiptoeing around the idea of living a bigger life, a scary bout of pneumonia landed me in hospital and brought me, briefly and blessedly, just close enough to death that I found myself saying, as my fever broke, "Fuck it, Universe. I'm all in."

That night, I picked up a pen and started writing poems, something I hadn't done since, at age 15, I'd gathered all my writing into a box and put it –literally and metaphorically- under my bed to focus on important pursuits like boys (what a dupe!), school and a career.

Now it was out of my control. I leapt naked from the tub to write. I would wake to poems I'd forgotten I'd written, finding them on scraps of paper in strange places.

Half-baked thoughts. Confessions. Ideas. Descriptions. Observations. Questions.

I began to share them with others, walking that razor's edge between having to divorce myself from how they may be received and also hoping they made the reader feel something. Every time I posted or shared my work, I would get a headache, or the shakes, or feel sick in my stomach. I still do, no matter how many times I do it. Vulnerability hangovers are real, y'all.

But I came to realise it wasn't the idea of judgement that I was actually scared of. It was the fear of being selfish. Of doing something I loved for no other reason than the fact that I love it. In my work with women, I know this to be a collective experience- this fear of being selfish- which is why I often prescribe participating in some kind of creative pursuit as part of my work with clients.

Creating art for the sake of creating art is a sublime way of giving air to the parts of yourself that have withered. Sharing it with others forces you to confront your greatest fears. Deciding that your own work is good enough is a powerful act of self- love and self-actualisation.

A crash course in becoming whole.

So my hope for those of you reading this book is this:

I hope you like these poems.

I hope they make you feel something.

I also hope they inspire you to write your own poetry.

To distil your memories into sensations in your body and then translate them into words, bringing them to life when you read them aloud.

The democratisation of the arts through avenues like social media (bemoaned by those who profit emotionally and financially by deciding who has access to the right to call themselves an artist) means that the gatekeepers have fallen. Indeed, you can bestow the title of poet upon yourself simply by including it in your Insta handle.

And at this moment in time, isn't that we all need more of? People who are brave enough to show up and be fully human by sharing their thoughts and emotions? Isn't it being reminded of the collective experiences- of love, loss, grief, ageing, joy, pain, sadness, anger- that helps us rise above the divisions?

I think so.

So indulge yourself, friend. Do the things that make you feel better (even if just for a minute) and find the courage to share it with others, so that they might be inspired to do the same.

Big love,
Meghann

A Revelatory Tale

(Or Things They Do Not Tell You About Letting Yourself Go)

I did not know that when I stopped waxing,
plucking, straightening, colouring, weighing,
measuring, judging, caring and- as they say-
let myself go,

that it would feel like pieces of me were
falling to the ground as my hands,
clenched so tightly for so long,

unfurl, soften, open,

palms to the sky as if to receive,

And I would know what unburdened meant.

I did not know that all those spaces in my
body where fear had built barricades
with ideas and programs and diets from
women's magazines would suddenly be opened

And I would know what expansion felt like.

I did not know that my mind-
who'd been driving the same car around
the same streets in the same direction for
decades, following ALL the rules-
would suddenly swing a hard left and skip
town, heading for the highway,
windows down,

And I would know anticipation.

I did not know that the sight of my face in a
mirror- changing, softening, crinkling-
would someday startle me so much that I
would want to cry,

not in mourning for the girl I can no longer
see, but in recognition that each line has been
carved by experience, and wisdom, and laughter,

And I would know respect.

"Don't let yourself go!" A warning.

"You've let yourself go!" Hurled as an insult.

But if you close your eyes and hold your face in your hands, heartbeat in your fingertips, take a deep breath and sigh as you

let
yourself
go?

Then

it becomes an invitation

to a life that is only just beginning.

Enough

Enough.

Enough ignoring the too long hug of your
friend's husband or your uncle or that guy at
work whose hand lingers on your hip in a way that
makes you ache,

while you convince yourself to be grateful
that people still find a Woman Your Age
attractive, rounding your shoulders forward,

shrinking

until your breath is shallow and fast.

No, sister.
Stand up. Push back. Breathe.

Enough.

Enough diminishing yourself by saying,
Oh, I haven't washed it in days! or
Yeah, but it's not as good as yours/hers/theirs... or
No. Really?, voice rising in a question while you blush,

No, sister.
Speak up. Say thank you. Receive.

Enough.

Enough saying how lucky you are when what you are- what you are ALLOWED to be- is proud,

because your life, your family, your career, your creations, your offerings, your soul is not the result of luck,

They are the result of focus. Discipline. Fear. Doubt. Effort. Courage. Blood. Sweat. Tears.

Of picking yourself up again and again and again knowing that there is another punch coming and it will catch you square on the jaw or in the gut and you will fall.

No, sister.
Rise up. Lower your stance. Go again.

Enough.

Enough of the shoulds and have-tos and I can't
and not my place and stay small and don't stand out
and be nice and be quiet and shhhhhh...

No, sister.
Burn up. As hot as the sun. Shine.

Explode.

When They Howl

When they howl for you, will you come?

Maybe?

Maybe not.

Look, I understand the hesitation.
This isn't a trip you had planned and
that bag you're carrying looks heavy,

And surely it is, with a thousand years of
shame and fear and half eaten dreams
weighing you down,

Pretending to not know is exhausting.

And looking the other way all the time for a
more convenient explanation or a reason not to hear
is bad for the neck, not to mention the soul,

But you can put it down.

That bag is full of things you do not need.

We travel light from here on in, because the
place I am taking you has everything you need,

The She-Wolves there- though wild- are nothing to fear.

Underneath their fur, they are soft and
gentle and longing for you,

but also, like all women, they have shit to do
and are growing impatient, each snap of their jaws
a reminder of the following:

They're hungry.

Maybe is not an answer they will accept and they
are growing restless, circling the fire,
awaiting your response.

So you must feel now, into your bones, your flesh,
your deepest parts, the shadows where You are hesitating,

and when you open your mouth to answer,
do not be alarmed at what spills forth, be it
rage or grief or song or joy or silence or blood,

For any of it- all of it- will be transformed
into a breathless, dripping "Yes"

a murmur of swallows on an early evening flight,

carrying your devotion to the beasts who
have set a place at their table and are saving
the best parts of the kill for you;

The guts are all yours.

Stardust

For so many years I bemoaned my thighs.

The shape of them, the width,
the sheer expanse of flesh,

and my stomach, too.

My hand would travel over the surface,
mouth twisting in distaste at the evidence
of my failures, pinched so hard between
my finger and thumb that it bruised.

But now I see it differently,
this place where I grew stardust,
whole people swelling in my womb.

Stretch marks, the aftermath of creation,
once angry and purple, now faded,

silvery, soft scars of remembrance of what I goddamn did.

Now when my fingertips play upon my waist,
my thighs, my breasts, my collarbone

it is with a soft, happy sigh
as I come home to the place
where life began anew.

A Knock on the Door After Dark

A knock on the door after dark always feels
ominous, more so when it swings open,
despite the fact that it was locked.

Imagine my surprise to find that all those
parts of me I thought I'd buried have returned now,

with matted hair and dirt caked fingernails,

to scratch at my door and bang on my windows until
I let them in so that we can dance and cry and sing and wail
and create and love and surrender

Together.

All those parts I deemed not safe for public consumption
have been hungry for so long that they have nothing to
bind them to the niceties that kept them
chained and contained and controlled,

All those parts I locked in the cellar to keep them
from being seen now sit unflinchingly
beneath the interrogation light,

staring directly into the glare until
they are blinded by their own boldness.

All those parts of me I starved of love,
of food, of oxygen, of acceptance,

have only grown bigger than before,

biding their time until now when they knew
that I too would grow bigger

and be brave enough to let them all in.

How Jarring It Is to Look Into the Mirror

How jarring it is to look into the mirror
and see my mother's face,
to hear her voice when I speak,
to see her hands when I fold mine in my lap
(though hers are always softer),

To feel the thread that binds us so tightly together
as it trails off in both directions, to the women
who came before and those who have not yet been
birthed into existence by the Great Spirit,

A thousand faces, smiling all at once

at the things they remember
the things they know
the things they will bring to pass

and laughing at me (just a little)
every single time I think I have it all figured out.

This Middle Aged Rage

This middle aged rage is fuelled by sugar,

I know the pairings well.

Chocolate cake with a sliver of disappointment,
extra icing to coat the resentment.

As if enough sweetness can nullify the bitter taste
that seems to be always present,

twisting my mouth and deepening the wrinkles.

Oh! The wrinkles!
Shortbread for those.

Chew, chew, chew. Swallow.

Feeling all that misplaced anger settling in
my gut the way the glitter in a snow globe eventually sinks,

but I feel like I am always being shaken.

*　*　*

You wanna go? Let's go.

I hear the words in my head and flush,
running my tongue over a tooth I chipped grinding my teeth,

(Don't even get me started on dental fees.
Those require alcohol.)

*I almost got into a fistfight today at the shop*s, I tell my friend,
who laughs- a real laugh, hearty and from the belly-
and then says, *Really? You?*, voice rising at the end,

Making me wonder if they would give me an
Oscar for Outstanding Performance of a Woman
Who Seems Fine but is Totally Not Fine
before she adds, *Yeah, actually. I can see it.*

which makes me feel suddenly,
and absurdly, proud.

See? I say to myself. *You've not gone soft.*

*　*　*

I tell her that I didn't start it but that I didn't back down
and that what surprised me more than anything was that
when I got into my car, there was no rush of adrenaline,

only a vague, empty feeling that it took me a
minute to recognise as disappointment.

I wanted to fight the woman who almost hit me with her car,
who continued to scream obscenities even after I'd apologised,
whose rage had clearly not been sated by baked goods.

* * *

But instead I came home and distracted myself
with meeting the demands of others,

all the while trying to appease the Beast in my
belly with promises that I would let her out soon,
while she laughs with glee at the thought of her freedom
in a world where all the constraints have been felled by
what I would like to think is confidence, even wisdom,
but is more likely sheer exhaustion.

Until then, she waits,

asking me if I can make another batch of my
grandmother's fudge, which I do,

smoothing it into the pan

with a hand that won't stop shaking.

Sturdy

I want to feel sturdy in this body,

slapping my thighs with pride and gratitude
for the way my legs ground me to this extraordinary Earth.

I want to love the solidness of my body the way
I love the solidness of the giant, ancient oak
that stands in the front yard.

I want to revel in my body's softness the way
I savour the absence of edges when I press
my face into my lover's neck.

I want to feel graceful in this body,
able to move and love and dance in a way
that shows a piece of who I *really* am
beneath all this fuss that comes with being human.

I want to feel familiarity in this body;
intimate with every nook and cranny,
knowing the story behind every scar,

feeling unshakeably like I belong,

each time I allow my
wondrous, grateful breath
to bring me home.

Wild Thing

I am a Wild Thing.

Though I spent most of my life trying to
beat myself into submission,

filing my claws,
biting my own tongue until it bled
to keep myself from growling.

You are a Wild Thing.

Though you have forgotten how to crawl,
to climb, to swing from vines;
knees and hips stiff from too much time
sitting with your legs crossed,
following the rules.

Come with me,

let us be Wild Things together,

so that we can remind each other how it feels
to run with the pack,

shaking the Earth,

flashing our teeth,

howling as one at the moon,

louder and louder-

until the only voices we hear are our own.

Slightly Damaged And Totally Divine

I am spiritually clumsy.

Powered by a still beating heart filled with holes,
light spilling forth from the places
that fear and loss have punctured

radiating and receiving life with every single thump,

Wearing a crown that has seen better days,
missing some jewels,
cracked where it was dropped in battle;

tarnished,

yet all the more beautiful because every time
I pick it up and put it back on it is easier
to bear the weight,

and know that

while I, too, am most certainly slightly damaged,

I always have been- always will be-

totally Divine.

Two Women

Two women. Two wombs.

One bleeding, emptying,
taking with it the baby she'd hardly
dared hope for after all this time,

The other swelling; filling with a life
she did not plan for and does not want.

Hands shaking, wiping the tears from each other's faces-
It's OK, it's OK, it's OK.

sick with anger and the unfairness of it all,

their pain entwined so deeply they can hardly
tell where their own begins and ends,
so they bear it together, breathing as one,
through a grief that is tearing them apart.

Reckoning

I wish for you a reckoning;

a dark night of the soul that feels neverending

a black that seem impenetrable

a moment that finds you on the floor, wailing,
"Who am I? Who am I? Who am I?"

Perhaps it seems cruel that I would invite
such a crisis upon you but hear me out.

I wish for you a reckoning because I know that sometimes

in the dark night you learn to see without your eyes

in that deep black you learn to hear

that in that moment of seeking the truth of
who you are you realise the question can
never be answered because *you* don't really exist at all.

I wish for you a reckoning;

because when everything falls apart
and you are left cracked open and raw,

it is then that sensation overwhelms thought

and you can finally feel your way back to yourself.

Eve; Reimagined

What if Eve had eaten the snake, instead,

before he told her that the apple was forbidden

so that when she did, eventually,
get round to having a snack

all she would have ingested was a deep, deep knowing

without a side of shame?

I Am Loving Myself Whole

I am loving myself whole,

bit by bit,

with each mouthful of food that bears no consequence,

each glance at a mirror that sparks a smile and not disgust,

with each conversation that starts with a giant, shuddering breath and ends with decades of shadows dissipating like fog when the sun finally burns through.

I am loving myself whole with each

"No."

and

"Stop."

and

"Fuck off."

and

"Yes."

and

"More."

With each beat of a heart allowed to want what it wants and a voice that is learning to ask for it.

I am loving myself whole each time
I pull back another layer of the Not Me
to reveal a core that is both delicate and strong,

complete in its nature,

to which expectation cannot bind.

There is Joy to Be Had

There is joy to be had,

in the soft slap of flesh allowed to sag,

the sigh of my thighs as they relax, and open;

when I let the tension make room for existence.

There is joy to be had,

when I stop trying to be anything but
what I am in this moment,

yearning to sink into myself.

Climb

I am always so angry with myself
when I realise that I gave up climbing trees
to spend my time worrying about boys,

a grave loss of perspective I am climbing out of now.

Though I am less monkey; more sloth,

I have been pleasantly surprised to find that
I still have little fear of heights.

Oh Captain, School Captain!

As she delivers the welcome address at the College's
Open Night and shares her hopes and dreams for
further education, a career, a life, I can see it on her face-

the unwavering belief that *this is how it will
be* because she's got it all planned out, you see,
and the train has to run on schedule.

I want to tell her not to panic when she is derailed

by unexpectedly falling in love

or a hundred decisions made under duress,
and pressures she will not name for decades,

new opportunities she can't possibly
imagine because her world feels so big at 17
but is still, in fact, quite small,

and a world that will insist it heard "Yes!"
while she was screaming "No!"

by children she will love but who do not -surprise! -
nap quietly while she goes back to work,

and finding out they gave her job away, then
realising she hated that job anyway.

I want to tell her that when the train goes off the track,
she doesn't need to wait for the emergency crew who
will drape her in a blanket and tell her what do next
to stay safe

and that, sometimes,

fleeing the scene is the quickest back to yourself.

If I Could Swallow Fire

If I could swallow fire,
I would ask it to burn through me,

and seek out every bit of rotten wood
that I used to build bridges to destinations
I never really wanted to explore/
the scaffolds I have used to prop up
identities that no longer fit/
the boxes I hammered together so that I
could climb inside and feel safe/
the reinforcements I have layered over my heart
through decades of trying to protect it, as though
boarding up windows as a tornado bears down.

Burn it all, I would ask,

but leave the ashes smouldering so that
if I need to, I can swallow them again
and set aflame the structures that confine me.

Wonder

(A Commencement Address)

As an esteemed alumni of the School of Hard Knocks,
I offer you this:

It will all be OK.

Maybe not grand or exciting,
the way you had hoped,

There will be sadness. You will feel very scared.

Kid, it's gonna hurt.

But crouch down here in these blades of grass;
there are tiny pebbles of wonder you can roll
between your fingers until your breath is calm.

A smile, perhaps.
The smell of coffee and woodsmoke.
Your favourite book.
Your son's laugh.

Pick them up now and pinch them
so hard they leave a mark,

Put them in your pocket so when you are
old and tired from all the goddamn tragedy,
wondering if you can take another step,

you will be able to run your fingers through
all those stones and remember that you are
weighed down by love.

What Story Do You Tell Yourself?

Ahem, excuse me...
may I please have your attention?
I have something to share with you
and it bears more than a mention.

Now I know I may not look like the kind of
woman who spits rhymes,
and you'd be right, I really can't,
(well, not the way Cardi B. does all the time),

But I can fuck your brain and
create a story in your mind,
by using words- it's easy!-
we do it all the time.

Now if you would, please close your eyes,
this'll only take a minute,
and picture now an elephant
cuddling with a kitten.

It's so absurd, what I just said,
and yet you all just saw it,
and now that image lingers there.

Imagination, inconvenient.

All day long you do the same,
paint pictures with your mind,
but what I said was funny
and most certainly not unkind.

What story do *you* tell?

* * *

What story do you tell yourself?
Your family? Your lover?

What story do you tell yourself?
And could you choose another?

Are you taunting? Are you cruel?
Serving judgement all the time?
Do you belittle yourself so badly
that sometimes you want to die?

Are you careless with your thoughts and words,
the stories that you tell?
Ignorant and unaware that they saturate your cells?

And they keep you small and lonely,
these stories that you write,
Shrinking this grand and glorious world
down to the size of your thighs,

Grinding, grinding, grinding
on your pure and loving soul,
Until all that's left are ashes and
you're slowly growing cold,

So we try so hard to warm ourselves
in the light of our devices,
Seeking more and more while feeling less and less,

a slow death we invited.

Maybe this is why you find yourself,
when you open Instagram,
seeking love in likes and follows,
instead of holding it in your hand,

And maybe that's why you choose the
same goddamn filter every time,
the one that makes you look like stardust,

Ethereal.

Divine.

* * *

And maybe you don't choose it because it's what you
wish you looked like now,
maybe it's because part of you knows it's who you are,
it's who you've always been, and that longing you feel
to change your face, your hair, your body, your life,
is only there because you have forgotten that YOU
are a cosmic being on a giant rock floating in space.

* * *

So what if that, my love, was the story that you told?
Of love and awe and magic, and the joys of growing old?
Stories that will celebrate the miracle that you are?
The broken parts, your tummy, and every singe scar?

What if, instead, you spoke to yourself
as if you were divine?
Worshipping yourself with narratives
you know are true and kind?

Now think again of the elephant and his beloved feline friend,
how easy it is to make things real by thinking them in your head!

And listen up to what you say,
There's power in your words,
Whether nice or nasty,
Your story will be heard.
Again and again, day in, day out,
You shape who you will be,

Let the words you conjure- manifest-
be ones of poetry.

This Grief

This grief is like mud in my hands,

Loamy and black,
warming to my touch and slipping
through my fingers as I try to shape
it into something familiar,

a thing I know how to hold.

But even as I sink further into it,
surrendering to its weight as it blocks out the lights,

my tears water the seeds that lie beneath the surface

and new life unfurls toward the sky.

The cycle begins again and reminds me
that Hope need not be cultivated,

it is feral; resolute; eternal.'

Treadmill (a haiku)

Going nowhere fast,

I pay good money for this.

I am fucking dumb.

I Was Raised by the Ocean

I was raised by the ocean.

Lulled to sleep by a foghorn,

not just the smell of salt in the air,
but the feel of it on my face;
a fine, crystalline layer on my skin that I would
wipe with my fingertips, then lick.

I was raised by the ocean.

Where classmates' fathers sailed on trawlers,
farther and farther away as the fish stocks
dwindled and wars erupted between
Industry and the Environmentalists.

I was raised by the ocean.

Where townspeople sometimes did not
return from the sea, a funereal hush in the
streets as we waited for confirmation
before the names were added to the
monument in Town Square.

I was raised by the ocean.

So I know what unforgiving means,
and how you feel a thrill in your stomach
when dark blue waters turn grey, then black.

I was raised by the ocean.

So I know, too, that it will ebb and flow forever,
breakers crashing onto the shore,
thump thump thumping in time with my heartbeat
as the tides expand and contract in my veins,

so that even when I am perfectly still I am always-
almost unbearably, in motion.

Swiss Army Soul

Do not allow yourself to become so entangled in the

Coulda
Shoulda
Woulda
If only
Might have been but never was

that you forget your Swiss Army Soul has
at least 17 ways to cut yourself free from all those (k)nots

most of which weren't tied by you in the first place.

Take a deep breath,

flick open the switchblade,

and find out what it means to be

Untethered.

Psych Ward

On the geriatric care unit, his wife brings
him fried clams and a soft serve ice cream
from the Dairy Bar every Sunday,

and spoons it into his mouth as he smiles at her,
asking again and again what her name is and saying,
"How did you know these are my favourite foods?"

I switch my shifts to the psych ward

because my heart finds it easier to bear the violence
than to watch her face as he asks her who she is
and she wonders if she even knows the answer anymore.

Antidote

When I am brokenhearted,

I listen.

For the sounds of birds, and the wind,
and the cars on the road,
reminding me that even though I feel
like my heart has gone MIA
I am, in fact, quite intact
(despite my best attempts to disintegrate).

I listen until the fear of missing out
overwhelms my desire to stay so sad,

until the sounds I hear draw me back
into the busyness, the chaos of living.

I listen,

and then I clear my throat and sing.

Undammed

All this time I thought the salt water
I could taste was my tears,

until I realised

it was the river within,

at last undammed,

carrying my grief to the sea.

Waiting for Later

While you're waiting patiently
for Later to knock on the door,

delivering a polite and timely heads up
that you'd best get on with living,

Too Late is seeping its way through
the cracks in the basement,

wending its way into the attic amongst the ivy,

heaving rocks through all the windows at once.

And you, with the nerve to act surprised-

as if that security system you installed
could ever have stopped the invasion.

Doris

At Fred's Pancake House we pooled our spare change
to buy the Endless Stack for sharing on Sundays

which was, of course, against the rules.

But the waitress- a woman named Doris-
was either kind or being paid too little to care and
she'd let it slide, refilling our coffee mugs,
whipping a Bic from her apron to light our cigarettes
as we laughed and cried over problems I can't remember now.

Maybe she knew what it was like to be
young and hungry, or maybe she was bored,

But whatever her motive she taught me
to add salt to the coffee grounds,
that extra maple syrup is always a good idea,
a Prairie Oyster was a miracle cure for hangovers and that,
no matter how much I thought I liked him,
no boy was ever worth that many tears.

Coughing into a tea towel, she'd wave her smoke
into the air and swear she was gonna give em' up
but we all knew she never would,

and on the weekend after graduation she served us beans
and sausages along with our usual and told us it was
on the house while Fred glared at her from behind the grill
until she flipped him the bird,

then waved us off from the parking lot,

blowing perfect rings of smoke into the cool
morning air that was only just beginning
to swell with the promise of spring.

Psychic

"You've not got long left," she says, nonchalant.
"Two years, maybe three."

and even though the woman is a psychic,
not a doctor, and I know a real seer
would never put a number on it

I flush,

and find myself that night serving dinner on the good plates,
looking at the stars in the sky,
and laying with my boys for hours until they fall asleep.

The next morning in traffic a man cuts me off
and I don't even yell "Dickhead!"

a new, calmer, beatific version of me in the driver's seat,

making me wonder if maybe, just for kicks,
the psychic gives all her customers a
truncated life sentence so that,
with whatever time they do have left,

they're just a little more alive.

Umbrella

If you see me carrying an umbrella

wrestle it from my hands

and remind me that I'm not the kind of woman
who prefers dry clothes and comfort

over a thousand sudden kisses from the sky.

The Audacious Berry

Oh!
The audacity of this berry to grow in the winter,
a time of sleep and death,

red amongst the barren.

Don't you know it's too cold?
Don't you know you've been neglected?
Don't you know you're the only one who
has ripened here on this vine,
nonchalant in your boldness?

Perhaps an oddity.

Or maybe a reminder

of what can happen when we are
no longer governed by circumstance.

Solitude

Sometimes I long for solitude,
but I'll not have that here.

With each dip of my paddle, each splash of
water as I glide through my reflection on the lake,
I am surrounded.

This place is full of ghosts.

My grandfather, my great grandfather,
even my own father not yet dead,
come with me every time I launch my canoe.

They speak softly- and sometimes shout-
"Look, girl! Look at this place we have planted your roots."

They draw my attention to the hawk leaning slightly as it soars,

to the direction of the wind so I can adjust my course,

and always- always- to the rise of a trout.

Wildness

I doubt I can handle this Wildness.

It exhausts me-
a constant deluge of beauty
from first thing in the morning
until very late at night.

Mesmerised, I stay awake to watch the orange and reds
of the sky swim through the stars to the
pinks and purples of dawn,

and even while I sleep my heart keeps time
with the wind on the water,

the hoot of the owl,

the lonely, mournful cry of the loon.

Return to Earth

Lying on the shore, gazing at a treeline
as familiar to me as my own face,

I wonder;

if I just stopped moving, how long
would it take for me to return to Earth?

Minutes until the ants and blackflies and
mosquitoes would begin to feast.

Days (perhaps) until my flesh would begin to rot away
and the ravens get wind of the opportunity,
dropping bits of me into the lake as they fly away,
feeding the trout and snapping turtles and eels.

Maybe my limbs would be carried off by a coyote,

the beaver might use my bones to build a lodge.

I would not be left undisturbed, but become just another part
of life on the lake, my death nourishing a thousand lives,

and while my people would grieve, the land would not;

folding me back into its arms quickly, efficiently-
no mourning- and carrying me down to feed its roots.

This insignificance is astonishing and uncomfortable.

This world we've built with walls to protect us can't
keep us from knowing that Nature doesn't give a shit,

and when our time is up, we will return to this dirt
we bulldoze so we can be Bigger.

So numb yourself all you like:
with a bigger TV, or thicker soled shoes,
or a new A/C unit so you don't have to feel
the cycle of the seasons.

Build your fences; tear up the trees; pour concrete;
embrace progress!

She will watch you every moment,
unapologetic, impatient and hungry.

Nature will consume you the second you are dead,

and then, She will carry you home.

Hemlock

On the island I find the fallen hemlock,
mighty even in its sleep,

and spot the red Reishi blooming on its decay,

womb shaped, vibrant.

I drape myself on the log and watch
from the corner of my eye as a snake
slithers from beneath a fern,

undulating slowly, no sound, until it is stretched beside me.

As spores from the fungus burst and dance in
the rays of sunlight filtering through the canopy,

proliferating, wild in their urges to plant, begin again,

raining down upon my skin and reminding me
how it feels to be worshipped.

Surrender

Here in the ocean,

I let my breath take the lead,

allowing my body to settle,

remembering that it is only when
I surrender to the currents beneath,

that I no longer lose my balance.

My Grandmother's Kitchen

I will never forget my grandmother's kitchen,

the smell of the fire in the old woodstove,
the teapot stained with stories,
the plaid, woollen coat by the backdoor
that you wore when you needed more wood,
sticky with sap and scratchy against your neck
as you carried the logs in from the barn,

stamping your feet once, twice, three times
to knock the snow off so you wouldn't leave a puddle.

The spearmint leaves I stuffed into my cheeks,
chewing hard to the ticking of the clock,
eating as many as I could before my mum said "No more."

And checking every Royal Danish biscuit tin to
find the one that actually held the gingersnaps,

the kind I would remember the *pop* of opening
years later when an identical one filled with
needles and thread would reduce me to tears in
a church basement as I handed over a quarter
to buy somebody else's memory.

Green Beans

Snap, snap- plonk- as we top and tail the
green beans on the back porch,

I wonder if my grandmother knew that,
four decades later, I would still remember
the colours of her apron,

the hum of the bees in the lilac bush,

the itch of the mosquito bite on my leg
that I could not stop scratching.

An ordinary moment made extraordinary
because some small part of me knew -even then-
that memories like these could pry open your ribs

when grief makes you feel as if you
cannot take another breath.

Absurdity

On what would be their last trip to the woods,
my grandfather- hearing fading; eyesight failing- said,

"Ah, Donnie. This getting old stuff just isn't for me.
I hope when my time comes- BAM! [he punched his
fist into his palm for emphasis], God just takes me out.
None of this fading away."

A few weeks later, he was hit by a car and killed,

and when my father recounted this conversation
we laughed until we wept until we laughed again
before settling into silence,

dumbfounded by the absurdity
of this epic, cosmic joke.

Strawberries

When I was a little girl, I would eat all the
strawberries in my grandparent's garden and
then- covered in berry juice- swear up and down
to my grandfather that it wasn't me,

and he would say, "Well, then, must've been the chipmunks."

It never occurred to me that he knew the truth,
so committed to my happiness that he was the
one fooling me all along.

We would feed the pony sugar cubes; walk over the field
to the river; try to whistle after eating choke cherries,

my tiny hand engulfed in his huge, rough paw;

and this is why I know what it feels like when you're safe.

Roots

My mother says that when I
was born she had no instincts,

but I do not believe her

because she recognised, the moment I first drew breath,
that my big, tender heart would bear witness to much
beauty but would also make me a magnet for pain,

and so she taught me to grow roots-
down, down, down into the Earth-
and become unshakeable so that
when the storms of life battered me
I could not fly away from myself.

"Breathe, breathe, breathe- stay here, now," she would say,

and isn't that something we all need to know how to do?

ABOUT THE AUTHOR

Meghann Birks is a coach, creative, mama, lover and wannabe surf goddess living on the Mornington Peninsula. A magazine writer for over a decade, she is fascinated by the stories that we tell ourselves and the role of the arts in elevating our human consciousness.

This is her first book of published poems.

To stay up to date with events, workshops, coaching opportunities and publications, connect with her here:

www.meghannbirks.com

Instagram: @meghannbirkscoaching

www.ingramcontent.com/pod-product-compliance
Lightning Source LLC
Chambersburg PA
CBHW072014290426
44109CB00018B/2237